Dreams Into Reality

Manifest Your Dreams Into Being Using The Law Of Attraction

Thomas Calabris

Check out our website at:

www.InnerVitalityQigong.com

Dreams Into Reality
Publisher : Inner Vitality Systems, LLC.
Website : www.InnerVitalityQigong.com
ISBN : 978-1-951382-01-8

Copyright © 2019 by Thomas Calabris

Disclaimer
The Information presented in this publication is intended as an educational resource and is not intended as a substitute for proper medical advice. All readers are encouraged to seek proper professional and medical advice when needed. This book is not for anyone that has medical mental conditions. Do not read this book and seek proper medical treatment if you have serious mental illness.

The author and publisher of this material are not responsible in any manner whatsoever for any action or injury which may occur by reading or following the instruction in this document. The author cannot be held responsible for any personal or commercial damage caused by misinterpretation of the information or improper use of the information.

Dreams Into Reality

WHY YOU SHOULD READ THIS BOOK

There are many books written on the Law of Attraction, which all purport to teach about how to manifest the life of their dreams. However, many of these books are confusing, contradictory, and reveal the author's flawed understanding of the underlying processes involved. This book sets out to simplify and effectively explain the nature of the Law of Attraction and give the beginner all the tools necessary to apply it in their own life for powerful and positive changes.

Through several examples from humanity's greatest spiritual teachers, as well as cutting-edge scientific studies, the reader will come away with a profound and deep understanding of this universal law of life, which has the power to transform the individual radically from being a victim of external circumstances to the conscious creator of their own destiny.

This book will cover:
- The ancient history of the Law of Attraction, how humanity's greatest scientists and artists applied it, and more.

- What exactly is the Law of Attraction?
- The scientific basis and proofs for the veracity of the Law of Attraction in quantum physics and in psychology and neuroscience.
- A simple explanation of how our beliefs generate emotions, how emotions power our thoughts, and how our thoughts lead to actions – which create the reality we experience. In addition, how to choose our beliefs, emotions, and thoughts in order to consciously create the life of our dreams.
- Practical steps to help you define your true desire and intention so that you can manifest it in your life experience.
- How to understand the nature of abundance to attract to you all the money you require.
- How the Law of Attraction can bring you fulfilling relationships
- Utilizing the principles of the Law of Attraction to manifest perfect health
- Practical tips and strategies such as meditation, visualization, and affirmations to aid you in putting the LOA into practice.
- A four-step formula for the act of creation, which you can follow to create anything powerfully that you desire.
- How gratitude, prayer, and love is the key to success with the LOA
- Learn why living your highest joy is the means and the goal of your life, and receive guidance on how to live your passion in your everyday life.

WHY I WROTE THIS BOOK

I have studied and practiced Qigong in various forms for over thirty years. Qigong involves the study of energy as it applies to one's health and wellness, physical, mental, emotional, and spiritual. It is truly a holistic approach for living life and is a foundational cornerstone of Traditional Chinese Medicine. In Qigong, we often talk about the Chi (Qi) Field. The Universal Chi Field represents the energy and intelligence of all things. The Chi Field mirrors in ourselves and our lives the type of energy that we radiate outward by our thoughts, feelings, and actions. Thus, requiring the practitioner to train and condition their mind to focus on their desired intention to achieve positive results, in the form of relaxation, stress relief, self-healing, and healing others.

So why am I talking about Qigong when the subject of this book is the Law of Attraction? I believe the Universal Chi Field is the force and energy behind the universal law that has become popular these days and is known as the Law of Attraction. The similarities between the creative science of Qigong and the Chi Field and the Law of Attraction is the reason that I have decided to write this book.

Like the law of gravity, you can't escape the Law of Attraction. It affects you whether you're are consciously aware of it or not. The Law of Attraction is simple to understand, but it can take a lifetime of practice to perfect. The topic of this book is the Law of Attraction and from this point forward, there will be no mention of Qigong or the Chi Field. However, I believe that the Law of Attraction is important to understand for any life endeavor, including the practice of Qigong.

This book will give you a glimpse into the universal law that is becoming more popular and is being backed up by modern science and physics. The Law of Attraction has been around since the beginning of the universe. Once you understand what is possible with the Law of Attraction, you will understand that it is important to condition and train your mind to focus only on what you want, not on what you don't want. If you are looking for a way to take control of your life and looking for a way to attract prosperity, abundance, health, wealth, and love, then this book is for you. You will learn how to attract or manifest into your life your deepest desires and wishes. I hope you take the knowledge contained in this book and apply it in your life until your wishes and desires become your reality.

TABLE OF CONTENTS

INTRODUCTION

Everyone has wishes, dreams, and desires that they seek to realize, and for some, their life seems to unfold perfectly as everything they desire comes to them, while for others, they always seem to fail as they get the exact opposite of what they desire.

Why is this? Why do some people seem to effortlessly manifest and attract to themselves what they desire, while others seem to always attract negative situations? Are some people just destined for success and others destined for failure? Or do some people who are given what they desire, know some secrets that those who struggle do not know?

Whether they realize it consciously or not, the people who again and again in their lives find success in the fulfillment of their desires are following an ancient and eternal law. Historically, this law has been called many names, but in our recent modern world, it is known as The Law of Attraction.

While the Law of Attraction may be quite simple in theory, it can be very difficult to learn how to apply it intelligently to our lives in order to receive the outcomes we desire. This book will cover the essential aspects of this universal law and aid you in using it in your life in order to manifest your desires and dreams.

We will explore all aspects of this deep and powerful law of existence and offer some practical tips and exercises that you can utilize, to begin the practice of becoming a conscious creator of what you desire and a powerful attractive magnet of the things, which will bring you true joy.

In the following pages, we will be revealing ancient and eternal wisdom, which will explain the structure and mechanism of existence itself so that you may put yourself into intelligent alignment with the laws of life.

If you wish to harness the power of your consciousness to manifest your deepest desires and wildest dreams, then read on, and read carefully.

Chapter 1: What is the Law of Attraction?

"What you think, you create. What you feel, you attract. What you imagine, you become."

- Anonymous

Much is written about the Law of Attraction, yet many who teach how to use this principle never actually give a simple and clear definition of what it is and how it works. The Law of Attraction is a very simple law and very easy to understand. Perhaps it is so relatively unknown precisely because it is so simple and obvious. That law is essentially the universal truth that *what you put out is what you get back.*

The Law of Attraction works on the principle that the universe is made up of energy and vibration, and central to this "vibrational" universe is the fact that things of like vibration have a natural tendency to align themselves.

3

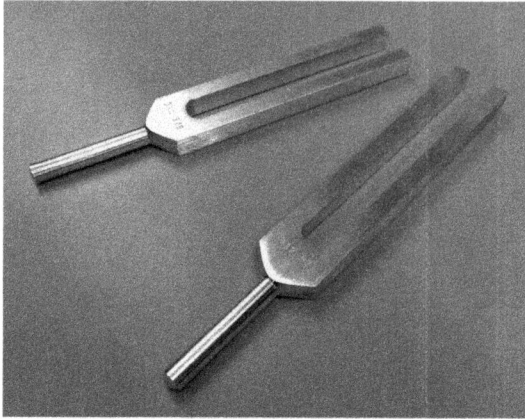

To illustrate this point, imagine you have two tuning forks tuned in the key of A across the room from each other. If you strike one of the tuning forks, the one at the other end of the room will begin to vibrate and produce a sound despite the fact that it was not touched physically. This is because these two tuning forks are of the same frequency. The first tuning fork vibrating in the frequency of an A note sends out energetic waves that are invisible to human perception but causes the second instrument to sound. This is a simple, yet clear example of the science of vibrational resonance and the Law of Attraction.

When this principle is applied to the human beings, it can be seen that for one individual who is vibrating and emitting energy of a happy and harmonious nature, they will vibrationally align themselves with these joyful outcomes and attract them into their life. Likewise, if an individual is having negative thoughts and emotions, then this is the signal they are broadcasting to the universe. The universe will send them the vibrational match of what they are expressing, and therefore, they will receive the fruits of their negative thoughts in the form of a real experience that they do not desire.

Charles Haanel wrote in his book *"The Master Key System"* in 1912, "The law of attraction will certainly and unerringly bring to you the conditions, environment, and experiences in life, corresponding with your habitual, characteristic, predominant mental attitude." [1]

Therefore, the person who observes this principle and consciously chooses their thoughts, emotions, and beliefs has seized the power to create their life as they wish it to be.

CHAPTER 2: THE HISTORY OF THE LAW OF ATTRACTION

Although The Law of Attraction has recently become quite popular with the publication of books such as *"The Secret,"* it is an ancient and ageless wisdom that has been known and put into practice by many of humanity's greatest figures.

The Buddha, as far back as 500 B.C., stated an understanding of the law when he said quite succinctly:

> *"All that we are is a result of what we have thought.*
>
> *If a man speak or act with an evil thought, suffering follows him as the wheel follows the hoof of the beast that draws the wagon.*
>
> *If a man speak or act with a good thought, happiness follows him like a shadow that never leaves him."*

In 391 B.C. the great Greek philosopher Plato wrote "likes tend towards likes," and as William Shakespeare correctly noted, "There is nothing either good or bad, but thinking makes it so."

You can also find some ideas that comprise the Law of Attraction in the Bible. In Proverbs 23:7, we find "As a man thinketh in his heart so is he." Also, Jesus himself referred to the universal law in many ways in the New Testament. For instance, in the Gospel of Matthew, he is quoted as saying "And all things, whatsoever ye shall ask in prayer, believe, you shall receive it."

More recently, in the 20th century, many books and teachings that have been influenced by the New Thought Movement and the Theosophical Society among others have taken the idea of the Law of Attraction and made it quite popular. One example of this is Napoleon Hill's *Think and Grow Rich,* which teaches of the power of the imagination, desire, and the subconscious mind to attract wealth and success to you.

In reading the words and reviewing the deeds of humanities luminaries one will invariably find references to the universal principles, which can be called the Law of Attraction. This is no accident, for whether they consciously realized it or not, this Law is central to our experience as human beings. Learning how the Law operates and how to align oneself with it enables you to create whatever you were born to accomplish in this world.

Chapter 3: The Physics of "The Law of Attraction"

"If you want to find the secrets of the Universe, think in terms of energy, frequency and vibration."

- Nikola Tesla

In the previous chapter, we showed how many great human beings throughout history have understood the Law of Attraction and used it in order to accomplish their great deeds. However, the origin of this law goes for much farther back than even the earliest of human society.

The Law of Attraction is a Universal Law

In fact, the law is older than humanity, as it is a fundamental law of existence itself. Even if humans were not able to understand or apply it intelligently, it would still exist and would operate unconsciously. Thus, being a foundational principle of the nature of reality, it needs no one's belief in it for it to be true and working. Just as the sun does not require your belief in it for it to rise every morning and set every evening.

Stated simply, the Law of Attraction is the formulation of a simple truth, that everything in existence is made up of energy in a state of vibration or frequency. The individual is also a vibrating field of energy, which magnetically attracts that which it aligns with energetically, while simultaneously repelling that which it does not align with energetically.

Therefore, what one experiences is only that which is a vibrational match of what they are; whether this is positive or negative outcomes depends wholly on one's own skill in becoming a pure transmitter of the frequency that they prefer.

One of the greatest physicists of the 20th century, Albert Einstein, understood the truth that there is truly no matter, but only energy that appears to the senses as matter. He said, "Concerning matter, we have been all wrong. What we have called matter is energy, whose vibration has been so lowered as to be perceptible to the senses. There is no matter."

It is similar to the tuning of an old-fashioned radio or television station. In order to receive the broadcast of a particular program, you must finely tune your dial in order to receive that program and not other programs. This television analogy aptly explains why the Law of Attraction has been stated as "like vibration unto like vibration".

If you are receiving the broadcast of channel 3, which is a horror movie full of conflict and sorrow, then you need to change the channel within yourself. You are receiving this movie because you tuned to its wavelength, so it has no choice but to be your experience. If, however, you decide you wish to experience a movie of a joyful adventure and loving friendships, you can shift your frequency from channel 3 to channel 4. Now that you have changed your internal broadcast signal, the external reality has no choice but to provide you with the movie that is commensurate with your internal state of being.

QUANTUM PHYSICS: EVERYTHING IS ENERGY

The Law of Attraction is simply energy physics, which explains how energy moves and operates in our reality.

Strictly scientifically-minded people often criticize the Law of Attraction as having no scientific basis. However, the fact that they would state this means that they either don't even really understand what the Law of Attraction is stating, or they do not understand the simple physics of energy. Actually, this universal law is quite easily proven scientifically.

The Double-Slit Experiment: Proof that You Create Your Reality

Everything is energy, therefore, we are made up of that energy too, and we actively choose our reality-experience based on what we give our attention to and align ourselves with energetically. If this is true, and more and more scientists are discovering that it is, then we have much more agency to dictate our reality than previously thought.

One very groundbreaking experiment that is causing scientists to significantly re-evaluate their models of the nature of existence is the double-slit experiment. This experiment reveals that our reality exists in an infinite field of possibility, and it is our active role as an observer, which collapses this infinite potential into what we call "physical reality." [2] Richard Feynman called it "a phenomenon which is impossible to explain in any classical way, and which has in it the heart of quantum mechanics. In reality, it contains the only mystery [of quantum mechanics]."

This experiment has proven scientifically that reality does not exist as something fixed outside of you, but rather that you are a participant in the creation of your experience of reality. It is one of many fairly recent experiments, in science which are forcing physicists to radically rethink everything they thought they understood about the nature of our universe and reality itself.

Chapter 4: How We Create Our Reality: Beliefs, Emotions, Thoughts, & Actions

"The universe is change, our life is what our thoughts make it."

- Marcus Aurelius

Now that we understand the basic physics, which underlie the Law of Attraction, we must now understand how to become a clear vibrational match of that which we desire so that it can be attracted into our lives and manifest.

Thoughts Become Things

Author Louise Hay, considered one of the originators of the idea of positive thinking, says the Law of Attraction is effective because "Our thinking creates and brings to us whatever we think about. Every time we think a thought, every time we speak a word, the universe is listening and responding to us." [3]

Our thoughts are magnetic, and our circumstances are the direct result of the thoughts that we think every moment of our lives. The thoughts in our head create the world we experience. Good thoughts lead to a positive experience, and bad thoughts lead to a negative experience.

Teachers of the Law of Attraction teach that "thoughts become things." Therefore, they teach that one must rule one's thoughts and only think positive thoughts in order to be successful with the Law of Attraction. While this is true, it is only *partially* true.

If you have ever tried to control your thoughts, you will know that it is very difficult to do. No matter how hard you try to think only positive thoughts, you cannot be vigilant all the time and inevitably, negative thoughts will creep in without you even noticing.

This is why in order to become a master of the Law of Attraction you must go deeper than thoughts and change your foundational beliefs and definitions, so that your thoughts naturally and effortlessly are positive and aligned with whom you prefer to be.

BELIEFS - EMOTIONS - THOUGHTS - ACTIONS

In order to become a powerful attractor and conscious manifestor of the experiences and the life you prefer, you must first become clear about and consciously define your **beliefs, emotions, thoughts, and actions.** These elements create your life experience, and an imbalance in any one of these areas will create a weakness in your total ability to create the life that you desire.

To understand the human being, it is helpful to recognize that the human personality construct is composed of four aspects. These are:

- Beliefs
- Emotions
- Thoughts
- Actions

Actions come from thoughts, which come from emotions, which come from belief. An imbalance or weakness in any of these four areas will lead to an inability to create or attract into one's life what you desire.

Everything begins with belief; this is the key to the whole structure.

You can't have an emotion without having a belief about the situation first. You only feel fear when you have a belief that what you are experiencing can harm you. If you believed or knew that you were completely safe, then you would feel no fear and would think no fearful thoughts.

We can represent this with the analogy of the building of a house.
- The **beliefs** are the blueprints, which are the designs of the house.
- The **emotions** are the builders whose energy goes into building the house.
- The **thoughts** are the building materials, whose quality will directly determine the integrity of the house.
- And the **actions** are the physical act of all of these elements being brought together into the act of making the house manifest.

If there is a deficiency in any of these areas, then the house itself will be structurally unstable. If the belief blueprints are faulty, then the house will be built in a structurally unsound manner. If the emotions/workers are not aligned, then there would not be enough energy to build the house or it would not be built well. And if the thoughts/materials are not clear, then the house will be built with poor materials and therefore be weak.

BELIEF IS REALITY

As we have just explained, while thoughts are very important in creating the reality we experience, they are merely the surface expression of deeper causes in our emotions and beliefs. If we trace the causes of our thoughts back to their source, they always begin in a particular belief.

Therefore, at the deepest level, we can say that reality is belief and belief is reality. For everything that we experience as our physical reality has its roots in our beliefs and definitions.

While there is an old saying that goes "seeing is believing", the truth is the exact opposite, "believing is seeing". This idea refers to the fact that our external reality does not exist as something solid and fixed, which exists outside of you, the observer. Rather, you take an active part in creating your reality based upon your beliefs and expectations.

Mind Over Matter: The Placebo Effect

More and more scientists are discovering the incredible power of consciousness and the subconscious mind. One great example of the power of our consciousness and mind to create the reality we experience is demonstrated by the placebo effect.

The placebo effect is the name for a fake treatment in the form of inactive substances, like a sugar pill, distilled water, or saline solution, which can sometimes improve a patient's condition simply because the person believes that it will be helpful. Numerous studies have shown the placebo to be just as effective as the drug that was specifically designed to heal an illness. [4]

For many years, scientists and doctors have been baffled that a patient is often just as likely to heal if they *believe* they have been given medicine as they are if they have been *actually* given medicine. Mainstream science has had a difficult time explaining this phenomenon and often would rather sweep it under the rug and forget about it. However, if they would look at it more closely and reflect on what the placebo effect shows in light of more recent discoveries of quantum physics, they would discover the incredible power of the individual to heal themselves purely through belief and expectation. That mind is truly more powerful than matter.

CONSCIOUSLY CHOOSING YOUR BELIEFS, THOUGHTS, AND FEELINGS

Now that we have understood clearly that our life is the result of our beliefs, emotions, thoughts, and actions that stem from them, we can take conscious control of these aspects of ourselves in order to create the life we desire.

As Marci Shimoff aptly says, "Once you begin to understand and truly master your thoughts and feelings, that's when you see how you can create your own reality. That's where your freedom is, that's where all your power is."

What we must learn is the art of **self-emoting,** which is consciously choosing your state of being no matter what the external circumstances happen to be. In doing this, we discover how not to become the victim of our circumstances, but rather choose to be a creator who has the power to choose our reality experience.

CONSCIOUS REALITY CREATION

The truth is that circumstances don't matter, only your state of being matters. This is a very simple but very profound truth. It means that there truly is no external reality, that the external reality is only a reflection of you.

The Law of Attraction teaches that the seemingly external, objective physical reality is actually not outside or separate from you at all. That is, it is actually a mirror that returns to you exactly whatever thoughts and emotions you are sending outward.

Therefore, if you wish to experience happiness and joy, then you must first become happy and joyful and then the external reality has no choice but to reflect this back to you. This is because the external universe does not have a mind of its own. YOU are the creator. If you change, the external world has no choice but to change to match you.

We can use the analogy of a mirror to illustrate this. If one is standing in front of a mirror, feeling sad, and they wish their reflection in the mirror to change to a smile, they would not take their hands and push the mirror, trying to force the image to change into a smile. They would simply move their own facial muscles into a smile and know and trust that the mirror will reflect this change of their state of being back to them.

This illustration is very simple, yet, many of us attempt to change the reflection in the mirror rather than changing *ourselves,* the source of the image. Many people say that they will only become happy if something changes in their life first. They say, "I will only be happy if I find my soul mate, I will only be happy if I make a lot of money," etc.

This perspective betrays a simple misunderstanding of the nature of reality. The Law of Attraction teaches us that we attract to us that which matches our vibrational frequency that we are emitting constantly like a beacon. Rather than attempting to struggle to bring about the things we desire in the world outside ourselves, we must first see to it that our signature vibrational beacon is purely expressing our true preference, and then the things we desire will have no choice but to manifest in our external lives.

CHAPTER 5: APPLYING THE LAW OF ATTRACTION

We now have a brief, yet deep understanding of the mechanics of the Law of Attraction and the nature of our reality. The next step is to take that essential knowledge of the nature of reality and how our experience is created and apply that in harmony with our passions, desires, and intentions.

WHAT DO YOU WANT?

What do you *really* want? This is such a simple question, yet, in our modern world of distractions and forces, which serve to keep us from being our true selves, it is often forgotten. As a result, many individuals spend their entire existence living in a pseudo-life, which is not what they really want but is what they are expected to be.

If one wishes to apply the Law of Attraction to manifest their desires, they would be wise to spend some time in contemplation so as to discover their true, deep, and lasting desire, not superficial desires that will not truly make them happy.

You certainly can utilize the Law of Attraction to manifest a shiny new sports car, but will that truly make you happy? Is that what your heart longs for? Or perhaps the desire for a nice, new car is actually a desire for something deeper.

There is nothing wrong with desiring to manifest material possessions, but the Law of Attraction is most powerful and effective when it is used to help one achieve the deep desire of their heart first and foremost. If this is accomplished, then all manner of forms of material abundance can manifest, but you are not attached to them and so they can actually manifest even easier.

As the great sage Jesus said, "Seek ye first the Kingdom of God and His righteousness, and all these things will be added unto you."

Take the time to deeply search within to discover what you *really* want. You may find that this deep dive into your interior to discover your deepest longing puts you into contact with the vibration of your desire, which as we now know magnetically begins attracting that reality to you.

LIVE YOUR JOY

We have learned about how our universe and our reality is essentially made from vibration, and the Law of Attraction is the expression of this vibrational multiverse in which things of like vibration are attracted to each other. In this vibrational reality, the higher the vibration, the greater the consciousness, energy, joy, and love. The lower the vibration the heavier and denser the experience, such as fear, sorrow, and pain.

Therefore, the more you live your joy and follow your deepest excitement the more and more your vibration will increase. This increase of your vibrational frequency, as you become more joyful will serve to bring you more of the things that bring you joy.

Excitement, passion, joy; these are all words for that which really speaks to your soul and provides you true happiness. And these feelings are actually your body-mind's translation of the feeling of living your true purpose, what you most love to do.

By living your passion moment-by-moment, you set into motion a spiraling vortex of energy that continually raises your vibration and brings you more and more of what brings you joy. This self-perpetuating cycle transforms you into a powerful magnet for the things you desire, which then allows you to keep acting on your excitement. Therefore, the key to getting the best outcomes from utilizing the Law is the act of following your passion and living in joy.

This is why it is of utmost importance that you act to the best of your ability to do whatever excites you in each moment. This does not need to be an overarching life purpose, but it can be in some people's case. It can just be something simple in each moment, such as the choice between reading a book or taking a walk.

Excitement is the thread that leads to all other excitement. By following it, you align yourself with who you deeply desire to be, which allows more and more excitement to be manifested in your life. Living your excitement is of vital importance. A person, who is passionately living their true joy, and is in vibrational resonance with what they desire, is a powerful manifesting force.

THE POWER OF INTENTION

Along with knowing what you truly desire and living your excitement, your intention is another key piece of the manifesting puzzle.

In order to manifest your desires, you must have a 100% conviction, without a doubt, that your intention will be actualized. The universe responds to your intentions. It is those with powerful intent that often see that they manifest their desires into being.

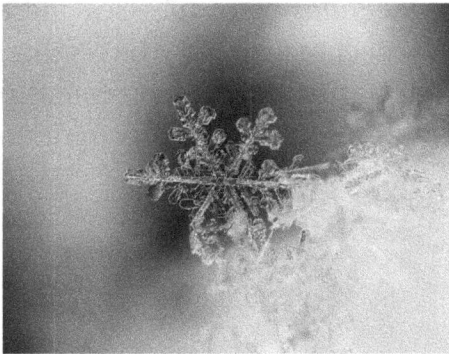

Stunning scientific support for the truth that our intentions and feelings have a profound impact on reality and the things we interact with, in our everyday lives. A Japanese researcher, Dr. Masaru Emoto, discovered this. In his experiments, Dr. Emoto took water and separated it into different containers. In some containers, he labeled with positive words such as "peace" and "love," while other containers were labeled with negative emotions and words such as "hate" and "disgust."

After quickly freezing the water in these containers, it was found that those, which were impressed with positive emotions, froze into beautiful crystalline patterns, while those associated with negativity froze into ugly and asymmetrical forms.

Dr. Emoto repeated these studies in many different ways in a variety of environments and always discovered this amazing connection between the intentions and feelings one expresses and the resultant effect upon physical reality. [5] His research shows in a stunning and beautiful way the profound power of our intentions, emotions, and thoughts upon the reality we experience.

Chapter 6: Key Considerations

"Most people are thinking about what they don't want, and they're wondering why it shows up over and over again."

- John Assaraf

Negative Law of Attraction: Attracting What You Do Not Want

The Law of Attraction could more precisely be called "The Law of Attraction and Repulsion". This is because calling it the Law of Attraction is only half of the whole story. The things that are vibrationally attuned to you are seeking to come to you, but it is also true that the things, which are not vibrationally a match, are doing their best to get away from you.

This is an area where many people run into issues. By not being clear in their beliefs, thoughts, and emotions about what they want and do not want, they often unconsciously are attracting the things they do not desire, while unconsciously repelling the very things they say they desire. Most people are unconsciously attracted to a mix of what they want and don't want.

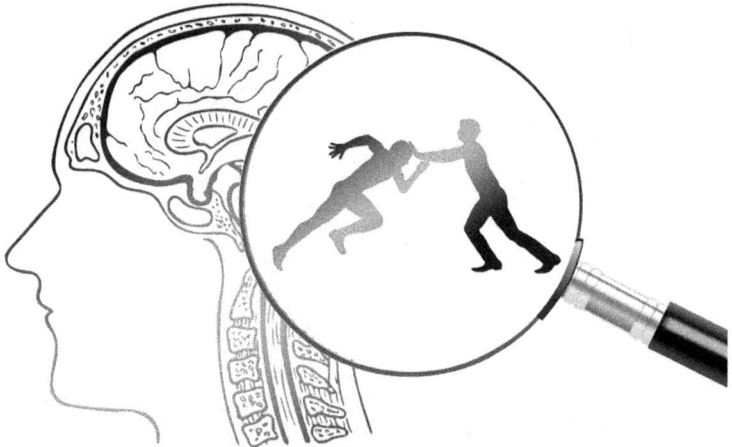

As Napoleon Hill advises: "Keep your mind fixed on what you want in life, not on what you don't want." [6]

This is why one must be very clear about their foundational beliefs and definitions, for one may think that they are being clear in their desire for something and are feeling the correct emotions and thinking the right thoughts to allow it to manifest, but there may be a hidden negative belief that prevents it from coming.

For example, one may desire financial abundance and do everything necessary to bring it forth in their life. However, perhaps they have a negative belief about financial success that is unconsciously blocking them from being wealthy. This is because, when they were young, their father pointed out a rich man who was also very mean and selfish. He told them that rich people are often not very nice people and "money is the root of all evil."

This created an unconscious association in the person's mind that one cannot be a wealthy person and a good person. Because of this negative belief, this person will never allow himself or herself to become rich because they would then have to become a bad person. Often the individual is not even consciously aware of having this type of negative belief.

In order to properly align oneself with the vibration of wealth and abundance, this person would have to recognize this negative belief and understand that it is simply not true; that one can be wealthy and be a very kind person. Only then will they fully allow themselves to allow wealth into their lives without any unconscious resistance.

SCARCITY AND ABUNDANCE

> *"Whoever has will be given more, and*
> *he will have an abundance. Whoever*
> *does not have, even what he has will*
> *be taken away from him."*
>
> *- Matthew 13:12*

Central to understanding and applying the Law of Attraction is in understanding the nature of abundance. As one of the most popular teachers of the law in recent times, Abraham, as channeled by Esther Hicks teaches, "Anything you can imagine is yours to be, do, or have." [7]

The idea is that, contrary to what most people are taught by our society, we are an eternal being living in a reality of infinite abundance. We are created in the image of The Creator, and therefore, contain the exact same creative freedom and power as that which is our source.

One who is skilled in living the Law of Attraction deeply knows that they are infinitely abundant and supported by the universe in the fulfillment of their desire.

It is important to understand that truly there is no scarcity unless you create scarcity in your experience. If you believe that you are not supported and that you don't have enough aid to be who you wish to be and do what you wish to do, then you will experience that reality. This is simply The Law in action.

What you focus on increases. Focus on scarcity and you will be given more scarcity. In a paradoxical way, you can see that what we call "scarcity" is actually an abundance, it is an *abundance of lack*.

In this way, you can see that you are always abundant, always given by existence what you are vibrationally giving out. But if you are not conscious of what beliefs and thoughts you are living with, you will lack, you will create an abundance of scarcity.

As we have already discussed, this highlights the importance of consciously choosing our beliefs and definitions, which serve you and allow you to manifest the reality-experience that you prefer.

THE SECRET TO THE SECRET: LETTING GO, AND LETTING IN

Many people believe the Law of Attraction to be difficult to understand and hard to actually live and apply it in their lives. However, the truth is that it is actually very simple and you don't have to learn how to do it.

You don't have to learn to attract or manifest, because you are always doing it and have always done it, whether you are conscious of it or not. You are ALWAYS already manifesting; you don't have to learn how to do it. Only consciously do it, cease to manifest what you don't want.

This is simply the way the universe and your consciousness operate. The things that are vibrationally compatible with whom you desire to be and what you desire to experience are always and constantly attempting to come to you. This is automatic and it is not something you need to learn to do. Likewise, the things that are not a vibrational match to you are doing everything they can do to get as far away from you as possible.

Knowing this, if you keep attracting things that you do not prefer, there must be something in you that is holding on to things that are actually trying to get away from you, and keeping away things that naturally wish to come to you.

"The true secret of the Law of Attraction is not "how to learn to attract" what you prefer, it's how to learn to let go *of what you don't, so that you can* let in *what is trying to get to you, automatically, by definition.*

That's the true secret, and that's why it's effortless. It's just about letting go, and letting in. It's not about having to learn to do something you're not already doing." [8]

- Bashar

As Bashar says, you don't have to learn how to do anything new. You only have to let go, relax, and allow in those things you say that you prefer.

Chapter 7: The Law & Your Life

*"Man, alone, has the power to
transform his thoughts into physical
reality; man, alone, can dream and
make his dreams come true." [9]*

– Napoleon Hill

There are a few common areas that individuals often wish to specifically apply the Law of Attraction to in their lives. We will go over these areas and explore how to use what we have learned to accomplish our goals in these very important aspects of our experience.

Money

Money is one of the most common topics, as it relates to the Law of Attraction, if not the most common. This is no accident, as money is the physical symbol in our world of abundance, energy, and the ability to have the freedom to obtain your desires.

What is money? It is simply a symbol and a token of energy. We often forget that the paper money we hold in our hands or the numbers in our bank account balance are abstractions, that they hold no intrinsic value in themselves. What they represent is energy. We do work that creates value for others and we are rewarded with money, which we can then use to exchange with others in order for them to create value for us. In this way, our entire monetary system is merely an organizational structure for the exchange of energy.

All too often, people struggle with money. What this really means is that they struggle with abundance and the ability to create energy and allow energy to flow through them. This is often due to limiting beliefs about their own abundance and ability to generate and receive the energies of universal abundance.

If you are inwardly abundant, then you will receive external abundance. Therefore, one who wishes to manifest monetary abundance must first become inwardly abundant. This begins with recognizing just how much riches you have within and are being gifted with by the universe at all times. As you do this, you will cease your miserly thought patterns and discover that there are countless opportunities to produce and share your value and others are glad to pay for the energy you are sharing with them.

RELATIONSHIPS

After money, relationships are perhaps the next most sought after desire. Unfortunately, once again people often seek relationships from a place of lack and scarcity. They desire someone to love them in order to fill up a lack of love that they are experiencing in their life.

It sounds cliché, but it is true. You must love yourself totally before you can attract someone in your life who will reflect that love back to you.

Our modern world all too often leads to individuals growing up without ever feeling unconditional love from their parents and guardians, and as a result, they don't feel unconditional love for themselves. They are taught that they are unworthy, that they are guilty of sin, and that they must find love outside of themselves. The truth is that if you cannot find love within yourself, you will never find it outside.

One who wishes to manifest loving relationships must first have unconditional love and respect for themselves. Then they are in a place of not needing love from an outside source in order to be fulfilled. And due to the unchangeable laws of existence, once you are inwardly abundant, you will be showered with more abundance.

This is the beautiful irony of life, that you will attract the relationship of your dreams only when you don't really care if you find someone to love you or not. Either way, you are content and fulfilled because you love yourself, and know that you are loved by existence, or God, or whatever you wish to call the higher power behind all of life.

HEALTH

Finally, we will briefly discuss the subject of health. In today's world, due to both external and internal factors, people are sicker than humans have ever been. We consume physical things that are poisonous such as unhealthy food, too much technology, and don't get enough sleep. We also consume psychological energy that is unhealthy from our media and the general culture around us.

All of these unhealthy and negative energies serve to make us tired and sick, which drags our vibrational frequency down. Negative thoughts are a damaging frequency and the more we indulge in them the more we likewise undertake negative actions with damaging consequences in our lives.

Physical sickness is a sign of imbalance. When we are ill, we are literally in a state of dis-ease. In order to apply the Law of Attraction in your life as regards to health, you must take responsibility for what you consume, for your daily lifestyle and change the things, which serve to cause your vibrational frequency to become low.

The more you align with the frequency of health the more you will receive the benefits of wholeness and harmony, which will allow you to become healthier in an ever-expanding circle.

BE THE FREQUENCY OF THAT WHICH YOU DESIRE

As have seen, with all of the previously discussed areas of life, where we wish to apply the Law of Attraction and manifest our desires, the key is in *being* the vibration of what we desire.

If we wish for financial success, we must think, feel, and act energetically abundant. To attract the relationship of our dreams, we must love ourselves without needing anyone else and then the universe may reflect our fullness back to us in the form of a friend or partner. To achieve perfect health, we must align our physical body, thoughts, and emotions with the vibration of health.

Regardless of the particular area of one's life, the mechanism of manifesting your desire is the same. This creation or manifestation process is what we will explore deeper in the next chapter.

CHAPTER 8: THE FORMULA FOR CREATION AND MANIFESTATION

Along with an understanding of the workings of the Law of Attraction, it is very useful to know the formula for creation. As the understanding that "like vibration unto like vibration" can be used in a comprehensive formula that gives a road map for how to create or manifest anything, you may desire, from the mundane to the miraculous.

THE FORMULA FOR CREATION/MANIFESTATION

There are many ways one can describe this formula. It can be described in five steps, or seven steps, or any number of steps. However, stated in the simplest form is, *See it, feel it, be it.*

First, you must imagine what you desire and be able to see it very clearly in your mind. Next, you feel what it would be like to have what you desire. Finally, you act as though it is so.

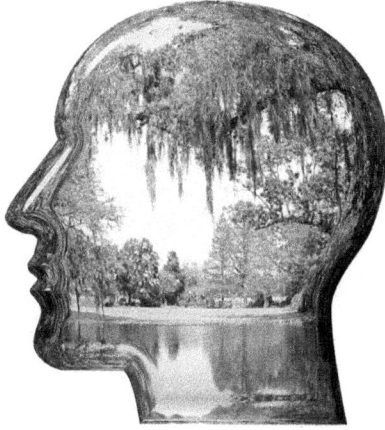

IMAGINATION: SEE IT

Albert Einstein, who understood the immense power of the imagination said, "Imagination is everything. It is the preview of life's coming attractions." We have imagination because without it we would not be able to create anything.

The imagination is the perceptual ability to command and manipulate realities that do not exist yet, because all existence begins first in seed form, in formless thought, and in the images of the mind. Therefore, imagination is actually what gives birth to reality, which gives reality to reality.

Everything begins first in the imagination before it is made manifest in the external world. If you can imagine it, you can create it.

"Imagination is the beginning of creation. You imagine what you desire, you will what you imagine, and at last, you create what you will."

- George Bernard Shaw

EMOTIONS: FEEL IT

After you have clearly seen what you desire, the next step is to feel it. You feel what it would be like if your imaged desire was already real. You should be able to feel all of the emotions that you would feel if it were so. Perhaps you would feel great excitement, gratitude, and self-empowered.

It is very important to totally feel all these emotions because feelings have the great power to make it real for you. To your subconscious mind, feeling that something exists is the same as if it were actually real. And as we already learned, as you put yourself into the same vibrational frequency of what you desire, that which you desire will be attracted to you.

ACTION: BE IT

The final step after you have imagined your ideal reality and felt the emotions of it is to take action and *be that thing*. In this step, you believe that it is possible for you to have what you desire and you put all of your will and intention into manifesting it.

You must act as if the thing you desire is already a reality for you and take the appropriate physical action. The key is to BE it. Don't *try* to be it. You must walk like it is so, talk like it is so, and think like it is so.

You must think and act as though you are the person who's desire has been fulfilled and essentially become that person. At first, this may feel strange. It is as though you are pretending to be someone you are not. However, the truth is that you can be whomever you choose to be.

You don't have to wait for the external reality to change in order to be a new person, you change internally first, then the external reality is merely a reflection that reinforces your inner transformation.

Action is the most important step because it makes something that is unmanifest, manifest. It signals to the universe that you are who you believe you wish to be. Action is the language of physical reality, therefore taking action grounds your intention into physical reality and allows the fruits of your imagination to take physical form.

Too often, people attempt to utilize the teachings of the Law of Attraction to manifest something, and they do a good job of imagining what they desire and feeling what it would feel like, but they don't take any action. Instead, they would rather wait for their life experience to give them what they wish for. In other words, they are waiting for external reality to prove to them that they have changed.

To get the full and true power of this formula you must take action. This is what completes the circle. It is a signal to the universe that you are whom you say you wish to be and are taking concrete physical action to manifest your desired intention.

BELIEF AND INDIFFERENCE

"If thou can believe, all things are possible, to him that believeth."

- Mark 9:23

There is one final element to this formula to make it truly powerful and most effective, and it is rather paradoxical. This final element is, that after you have put so much of your imagination, desire, intention, emotion, and action into manifesting what you wish, you should completely forget it and become indifferent. Another way of saying it is that you become detached from the desired outcome, whether it manifests or not.

To make this formula truly powerful, you must completely drop it, forget it, and be silent. This is a very subtle and difficult thing to explain. It shows the power of paradox, and that in any creation one must have a balance of opposites; light and dark, will and indifference, intense desire and complete surrender.

After the intense desire, belief, will, and taking the appropriate action, you completely forget it from your mind. This provides the other half of the polarity, the full circle. In our dualistic reality, you must have both elements to create.

You don't *need* it. You have no expectation and are in a state of non-attachment to the outcome. If you can find that place of contentment no matter what happens, then you have loosened your egoic grip upon your life, which allows your desire to flow naturally and effortlessly to you.

This also speaks to the effectiveness of gratitude and surrender. You are absolutely content with the way things are and have a deep trust that everything is already perfect. When you intensely desire something and at the same time you detach yourself from the outcome, you are demonstrating to the universe that you are open to receive whatever is in the universe's best interest.

At the highest level, you reach a point of high indifference where you really don't care if it happens or not. And it is this intense desire, yet unconditional detachment that you become available to the workings of grace.

CHAPTER 9: PRACTICES AND ACTIONS

"Ask, and it shall be given to you; seek,
and you shall find; knock, and it shall
be opened unto you"

– Matthew 7:7

In seeking to live the Law of Attraction in your life and use it to manifest what you desire, there are many techniques and practices you can experiment with. In this chapter we will highlight just a few potential practices, there are many more. It is suggested that you experiment with these and any others that appeal to your intuition.

All techniques and tools are like permission slips that can aid you in becoming more and more of your true self. Everyone will have different devices that will work best for their particular personality, so explore, and find what works for you.

MEDITATION

Meditation has been practiced in all cultures on earth for all of human history because it is the most effective way to calm the overactive mind and access deeper levels of your consciousness. It can benefit anyone who is seeking to practice the Law of Attraction and manifest his or her desires.

The practice of meditation allows you to sink deeper into your true self and bypass the static noise of the superficial thinking mind, where you can then access the deeper wisdom of your heart and your higher self or soul.

You do not have to have any strict or regimented practice; simply start small with as little as five minutes a day of sitting in silence without any distractions. You can focus on your breath and the physical sensations around you, in order to not be sucked in by the ceaseless activity of the mind.

Once you have calmed your mind, sit and simply listen and feel. Become more open to the messages coming from your deeper self. You may suddenly get inspiration and ideas. With this, you can then begin to act on what you find in meditation in your daily life and be aided in your journey to manifest your dreams.

As you practice, you can gradually increase the time you spend in meditation. Just remember that a consistent daily meditation practice will yield the best results.

JOURNALING

Another powerful tool for tapping into the the Law of Attraction is the act of journaling. Through the process of putting your thoughts and ideas down on paper, you become better able to organize your thoughts and map out your desires.

There are no rules or guidelines on how best to do this. You can simply make mind maps or lists of what you desire, write down things you are grateful for, or plan out your dreams for what you wish to create in the future. The possibilities are endless and your journal is a sandbox for you to play and to allow your imagination to run wild.

AFFIRMATIONS

Affirmations are another powerful tool for aligning your frequency and changing negative thought patterns into positive life-affirming ones. They work on your subconscious mind and allow you to fundamentally change your deepest beliefs and definitions about who you are and what you are capable of accomplishing.

The possibilities for creating affirmations are endless. It is suggested that you write affirmations that are specific to the goals and desires you wish to actualize. Your affirmations can be broad and general or specifically geared for manifesting things like money, relationships, or whatever you desire.

You can write these affirmations down and read them throughout the day, post them up in your bedroom, or record them as an audio file and listen to them before going to sleep. Be creative and have fun with them. Trust that they will aid you in transforming your beliefs about yourself and your life.

Here are a few suggestions to get you started.

- Joy is my birthright; I exist to experience joy.
- I am a creator and I create with every thought.
- Anything that I can imagine is mine to be, do, or have.
- I accept my power.
- All experiences of my life are abundant and filling.
- Every experience I have is the perfect experience for my growth.
- I am worthy of love. Love is all around me.

CREATIVE VISUALIZATION

The final technique we will discuss is creative visualization. This is the powerful practice of closing your eyes and imagining what you desire to create or manifest.

To do this, you should spend at least 10 minutes allowing your imagination to explore and dream up anything you desire. Your imagination has no limits, so do not concern yourself with what is possible or practical. This is simply your time to be like a child, explore what you deeply desire, and allow yourself to believe that it is real.

You should explore every aspect and see the fruits of your imagination in every detail. For instance, if you wish to become a successful film actor, you can use this time to imagine yourself acting in your dream role. Allow yourself to picture every specific detail. How do you dress? How do you talk? What do you do when you go home from work? Where do you live? Who are your friends? This imaginative play can go on for a long time and you can increasingly add more and more details to your fantasy.

While our modern world often discounts the value of fantasy and imagination, it is actually one of our greatest gifts. It is the way in which we create new realities for ourselves in our actual physical lives. Numerous studies have shown that successful artists, athletes, businesspersons, and people of all walks of life often visualize their artwork, game, or important meetings beforehand and so are prepared for the real thing.

The power of visualization has been proven by numerous scientific studies. Demis Hassabis and Eleanor A. Maguire of the Institute of Neurology at University College London wrote in their paper, *The Construction System of the Brain*, "The ability to construct a hypothetical situation in one's imagination prior to it actually occurring may afford greater accuracy in predicting its eventual outcome." [10] Their research has shown that the more one visualizes a positive outcome for the future, the more likely that outcome will become manifested in their life.

As we stated before, your imagination is real and the things you experience while imagining are real for your deeper subconscious mind. This practice of creative visualization is the first step to making your dreams manifest. A consistent daily visualization practice will yield the best results.

CHAPTER 10: KEYS TO THE LAW OF ATTRACTION

Now that we have explored the nature and application of the Law of Attraction, there is one final piece of the puzzle to put into place in order to have the complete tool kit to create the life of your dreams.

This is the practice of tapping into the power of love, gratitude, and prayer. These states will allow you to greatly raise your vibrational frequency and align yourself with the highest power in existence. Thus, bringing you into a powerfully creative state of consciousness that is open to receiving the infinite abundance and power of one who is aligned with the universal will of life itself.

LOVE: THE MOST POWERFUL FORCE IN THE UNIVERSE

Many of our greatest sages, mystics, and poets have told us of the power of love. This is not just a poetic metaphor; love is literally the most powerful force in existence. One can say that it is the very nature of existence itself, that everything is made of love and from love.

Scientifically minded people say that everything is made up of matter. Physicists have discovered that matter is actually pure energy. Mystics and meditators say that this energy is more fundamentally light which is pure consciousness and that the nature of this consciousness is unconditional love.

If this is true, and it is suggested that you inquire within and discover if this is indeed the case, then by living in a state of unconditional love you align yourself with the highest power in creation and the source of all.

Many spiritual teachers attest to the truth that by living in unconditional love you are literally one with God or the source of everything. From this state of being, you are capable of working miracles and transcending all limitations. As Jesus says, "With man this is impossible, but with God all things are possible."

"The principle which gives thought the dynamic power to correlate with its object, and therefore master every adverse human condition, is the law of attraction, which is another name for love. This is an eternal and fundamental principle inherent in all things, in every system of philosophy, in every Religion and in every Science. There is no getting away from the law of love. It is feeling that imparts vitality to thought. Feeling is desire and desire is love. Thought impregnated with love becomes invincible." [1]

- Charles Haanel

Love is the most powerful force in the universe. It is the unconditional affection that existence has for itself. It is oneness recognizing itself as itself. If you wish to skillfully apply the Law of Attraction in your life to create the reality-experience you desire, then the practice of becoming more and more loving is essential. Living in and being unconditional love is both the way and the destination for you to raise your vibrational frequency.

GRATITUDE

Along with the practice and expression of living in unconditional love, gratitude is another essential practice and attitude to live in your quest. Gratitude is intimately connected with love; its distinction lies in that it is the practice of "counting your blessings" and deliberately feeling grateful for everything that you are given.

We must not forget, while we are seeking to obtain what we desire that we have already been given so much by our friends and family and by our life, existence, or God. If we try to obtain more without being grateful for what we already have, we run the risk of becoming greedy and allow our desires to control us. Then we may become a slave to our own ego.

By greedily grasping for more without being thankful for what we have, we block ourselves from receiving the blessings that are available to all. However, as we relax our desire and allow ourselves to feel how much we have already been given, we align ourselves with the vibration of abundance, which of course opens the gates for more abundance to flow.

Think about it like this. If you knew two little children and you gave them the gift of a toy, one of the children was very grateful and thanked you sincerely while the other one ignored you. Who would you be more likely to give a gift to in the future?

Gratitude opens you to receiving more reasons to be grateful. This is one example of the effect of the Law of Attraction operating in every aspect of our lives.

> *"Gratitude is an attitude that hooks us up to our source of supply. And the more grateful you are, the closer you become to your maker, to the architect of the universe, to the spiritual core of your being. It's a phenomenal lesson."*
>
> *- Bob Proctor*

PRAYER

Similar to love and gratitude, prayer is a state of being in which one is loving, open to receive, and thankful for what is given. The quality that makes prayer different yet connected to love and gratitude is surrender. Prayer is an open-hearted surrender to "thy will," not "my will."

While in a prayerful state, you may ask that you receive something from the universe or a higher power, but you do not demand it. Making demands or putting qualifications on what you desire takes you out of the receptivity necessary to be given what you request.

At the highest level, prayer is done with an assurance that simply by praying you are already receiving the fruits of your prayer. As Jesus says succinctly in the Gospels.

"Therefore I tell you, whatever you ask
in prayer, believe that you have
received it, and it will be yours."

- Mark 11:24

These three states of being of love, gratitude, and prayer are crucial to successfully utilize the Law of Attraction in order to manifest experiences that go beyond mere egoic desires. Through the practice of living more and more in these emotional states, you will enable your vibrational resonance and manifestation abilities to increase far beyond what is capable by one who does not live in loving gratitude. These states will allow you to be in harmony with the very essence and power of existence, and your life will be an ecstatic explosion of loving bliss wherein anything you truly desire you may receive.

CONCLUSION: DO WHAT BRINGS YOU JOY

"When I really understood that my primary aim was to feel and experience joy, then I began to do only those things which brought me joy. I have a saying: "If it ain't fun, don't do it!" Joy, love, freedom, happiness, laughter. That is what it is. Do whatever makes you feel that. Do the things that you love and bring you joy.

If you don't know what brings you joy, ask the question, "What is my joy? And as you find it commit yourself to it, to joy, the law of attraction will pour an avalanche of joyful things, people, circumstances, events and opportunities in your life." [11]

- Jack Canfield

In reading this book, you have been introduced to the Law of Attraction or the simple fact of existence that things of like vibration are attracted to one another.

You now know that through the understanding of this simple and profound law, you hold the key to experiencing the reality you desire through deliberate intent and the practice of aligning yourself with the frequency of that reality.

Understanding and living the somewhat counterintuitive truth of the Law of Attraction is a constantly evolving journey. This is not some simple trick you can do without fundamentally changing yourself and how you perceive reality.

Truly living and applying the Law of Attraction teachings means that you understand the truth that your real-life and your world are merely a reflection of your consciousness and the beliefs, emotions, and thoughts you hold to be true. Also, we become to realize that almost everything we are taught in our culture about the nature of ourselves and our reality is wrong and it disempowers us.

You are a divine creator who is one hundred percent responsible for the experience you are manifesting as "your life." You are completely free and completely responsible for what you experience because it is what you have brought to yourself through the nature of the frequency that you are expressing.

It takes time to truly understand this knowledge in the deepest levels of your being and become more skillful at ceasing to indulge in negative thoughts while becoming more and more a pure vibrational beacon of the things that you love and are representative of the true you.

My hope is that this book has aided you in understanding this fundamental law of existence and how simple and joyful it is to create and manifest the life of your dreams.

May you become a pure and powerful magnet of your deepest joy.
May you receive *exactly* what you put out.
For, of course, you always do.

REFERENCES

1 Haanel, C. (2007). The Master Key System. Filiquarian Publishing.

2 Greene, Brian (2007). The Fabric of the Cosmos: Space, Time, and the Texture of Reality. Random House LLC. p. 90. ISBN 978-0-307-42853-0.

3 Living the Law of Attraction. (n.d.). Retrieved November 1, 2019, from http://www.oprah.com/spirit/the-law-of-attraction-real-life-stories_1.

4 Howick J, Friedemann C, Tsakok M, Watson R, Tsakok T, Thomas J, et al. (2013) Are Treatments More Effective than Placebos? A Systematic Review and Meta-Analysis. PLoS ONE 8(5): e62599. https://doi.org/10.1371/journal.pone.0062599

5 Emoto, M. (1999). The Message from water. Tokyo: HADO Kyoikusha.

6 Hill, N. (2017, November 3). Keep your mind fixed on what you want in life, not on what you don't want. Retrieved November 1, 2019, from

https://www.naphill.org/tftd/thought_for_the_day_friday_no
vember_3_2017/.

7 Hicks, E. (n.d.). A SYNOPSIS OF ABRAHAM-HICKS'
TEACHINGS. Retrieved November 1, 2019, from
https://www.abraham-hicks.com/about/.

8 Beyond The Secret and into Abundance. (n.d.). Retrieved
from http://www.basharstore.com/beyondthe-secret/

9 Hill, N., & Pilarczyck, M. (2016). Think and grow rich.
Amersfoort: Invictus Library.

10 Demis Hassabis and Eleanor A. Maguire. The
Construction System of the Brain. Wellcome Trust Centre for
Neuroimaging, Institute of Neurology, University College
London, 12 Queen Square, London WC1N 3BG, UK

11 Byrne, R. (2018). The secret. New York: Atria Books.

ABOUT THE AUTHOR

Thomas Calabris has studied and practiced various forms of meditation and Qigong for almost thirty years. He studied meditation, Qigong, and Tai Chi from Grandmaster Robert Krueger. Most recently, he studied Inner Dan Arts Qigong (meditation and exercise) with Grandmaster Tianyou Hao, since January 2001. Thomas is a certified instructor of Inner Dan Arts Qigong. He also studied Qinway Qigong with Grandmaster Qinyin and Wisdom Healing Qigong with Master Mingtong Gu. He holds a Bachelor of Science Degree in Electrical Engineering and a Master of Science Degree in Biomedical Engineering. He is also a software engineer. He has also studied anatomy and physiology and various areas of natural health. He brings a unique perspective of science, tradition, and experience to his teachings.

Learn more about Qigong at:
http://www.InnerVitalityQigong.com

Learn more about stress relief at:
https://www.EliminateStressNow.com

OTHER BOOKS BY THE AUTHOR

Relax Your Mind: Simple Meditation Techniques to Relieve Stress and Quiet a Busy Mind

Learn more at:
https://www.amazon.com/dp/B07H1PMN62

Relax Your Mind Companion Workbook: A Guide To Learn Meditation Techniques to Relieve Stress and Quiet a Busy Mind

Learn more at:
https://www.amazon.com/dp/B07YRWVZSJ

Healing Stress: Effective Solutions for Relieving Stress and Living a Stress-Free Life

Learn more at:
https://www.amazon.com/dp/B07KVNXN14

The Color of Relaxation: Adult Coloring Book for Stress Relief and Relaxation

Learn more at:
https://www.amazon.com/gp/product/1086248295

www.ingramcontent.com/pod-product-compliance
Lightning Source LLC
Chambersburg PA
CBHW071837020426
42331CB00007B/1761